DEBORAH

By Pauline Youd
Illustrated by Elaine Garvin

SCANDINAVIA

People always came to Deborah for advice.
She had good answers to their problems.
"My wisdom comes from God," Deborah said.
"God loves me and protects me."
When the people came to Deborah,
she told them, "God loves you,
too, and will
protect you."

WHY WAS DEBORAH MAD?

The story about Deborah is taken from The Book of Judges, chapter 4.

After Ehud died, the Israelites once again did evil in the eyes of the LORD. So the LORD sold them into the hands of Jabin, a king of Canaan, who reigned in Hazor. The commander of his army was Sisera, who lived in Harosheth Haggoyim. Because he had nine hundred iron chariots and had cruelly oppressed the Israelites for twenty years, they cried to the LORD for help.

Deborah, a prophetess, the wife of Lappidoth, was leading Israel at that time. She held court under the Palm of Deborah between Ramah and Bethel in the hill country of Ephraim, and the Israelites came to her to have their disputes decided. She sent for Barak son of Abinoam from Kedesh in Naphtali and said to him, "The LORD, the God of Israel, commands you: 'Go, take with you ten thousand men of Naphtali and Zebulun and lead the way to Mount Tabor. I will lure Sisera, the commander of Jabin's army, with his chariots and his troops to the Kishon River and give him into your hands.'"

Barak said to her, "If you go with me, I will go; but if you don't go with me, I won't go."

Then Deborah said to Barak, "Go! This is the day the LORD has given Sisera into your hands. Has not the LORD gone ahead of you?" So Barak went down Mount Tabor, followed by ten thousand men. At Barak's advance, the LORD routed Sisera and all his chariots and army by the sword, and Sisera abandoned his chariot and fled on foot. But Barak pursued the chariots and army as far as Harosheth Haggoyim. All the troops of Sisera fell by the sword; not a man was left.

Judges 4: 1-8; 14-16, NIV

Why Was Deborah Mad?

Published by Scandinavia Publishing House
Nørregade 32, DK-1165 Copenhagen K.
Tel.: (45) 33140091   Fax: (45) 33320091
E-Mail: scanpub1@post4.tele.dk

Copyright © 1997, Pauline Youd
Copyright © on artwork 1997, Daughters of St. Paul
Original English edition published by Pauline Books & Media,
50 Saint Paul's Avenue, Boston, USA
Scripture quotations are from the Holy Bible, New International Version,
Copyright © 1973, 1978, International Bible Society
Design by Ben Alex
Produced by Scandinavia Publishing House

Printed in Singapore.
ISBN 87 7247 048 8

All rights reserved. No part of this book may be reproduced or utilized
in any form or by any means, electronic or mechanical, including
photocopying, recording, or by any information storage and retrieval
system, without permission in writing from the publisher.

One day some people came and told Deborah they were being attacked. Their enemies took their land. Their enemies took their animals. Their enemies took their weapons so they couldn't fight back.

Their enemies took their land and their animals. They even made them slaves. That made Deborah mad! She shook her finger at the people.

"Don't let them do that!" she said. "Where are your strong men who will stand up for you?"

The people hung their heads. "We only know one man who has courage," they said.

"Go get him," commanded Deborah.

The people brought Barak.

"Go and fight the enemy!" said Deborah. "God loves you and will protect you."

"I'm afraid to go alone," said Barak, "but I will go if you will go with me."

That made Deborah *very* mad.

She shook her finger at Barak. "I will go," she said, "but a woman will get credit for winning the war. You will not!"

Barak called the army and fought against the enemy.

Deborah prayed to God and God helped Barak win the war.

Barak knew God loved him and gave him courage.

That made Deborah happy.

11

Did you ever know someone bigger and stronger than you who wanted to start a fight with you? What did you do?

If you pray, God can help you at times like that. He can give you wisdom like he gave Deborah. He can show you ways to make peace with those who start trouble. He can give you courage like he gave Barak. God will always show you the right thing to do if you ask him!

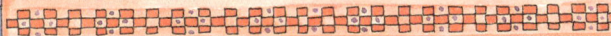

"Go! This is the day the LORD has given Sisera into your hands. Has not the LORD gone ahead of you?"
Judges 4:14

WONDER BOOKS
Lessons to learn from 12 Bible characters

God's Love

Self-giving

Prayer Overcomes Fear

Praising God

Prayer Obtains Wisdom

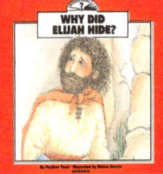

Listening to God

Trust

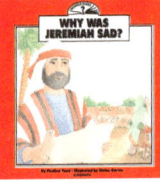

Perseverance

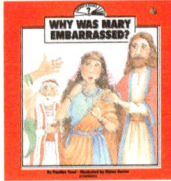

Loving Obedience

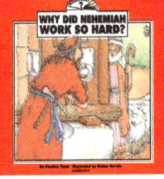

Persistence

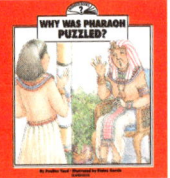

Asking Advice

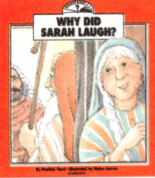

Trusting God's plan